WRITE AWESOME STORIES

Erin H. Thorn

For all authors

Believe in your talent
be inspired
live your dream
write your stories

The world needs them!

All of them.

1

WELCOME TO WRITING

Writing a book is simple. You have an idea and write it down, isn't it?

Well, unfortunately no, it isn't. Otherwise you wouldn't need this book.

With this book I want to give you a guideline a workbook how to write a book from scratch to finish. I will give you some needful sheets, some ideas and a direct contact line to me, if you need help.

Writing gives you the opportunity to free your soul, free your thoughts and create something you love. And if you get very good at it, there are actually a lot of people out there, just waiting for your story and what you've written. There will be people out there, who will pay to read your story and it will make them happy to read them. So give yourself a little nudge and try it.

I will help you along the way.

You might want to take notes, so you should have a pen ready. At the end of the book are 13 pages dedicated for your notes. If that is not enough or not the way you want to take notes, I recommend a notebook or anything similar while working with this book.

So first of all: you need an idea.
You need a good idea.
A good idea does not have to be the most elaborate idea there is. Keep it simple, but keep it interesting. If it is an over complex story, no one will get it. So just don't. Except you want to write art, but then: this book is not for you.

Keep it simple, but interesting.

2

FINDING YOUR IDEA

—————◆————

I hear you asking, alright, but where the hell do I find my ideas. I cannot give you the ultimate answer, but I can show you how others find theirs and how I find mine.

I get inspirations everywhere, literally everywhere.

When I walk in a car park, hear my own footsteps, I think of futuristic outlawed buildings, wars to be fought and one talented girl in the middle of all.

Or when I get myself some money at an ATM, I think, what might be behind it. What if the machine would slide away and reveal a world behind it, filled with alien beings living amongst us, helping us against all odds.

Sometimes, I get inspirations by pictures I see. A befriended photographer of mine edited a picture he took into a sea with red blood. Instantly when I looked at the picture, I had a trilogy in mind. A poisonous sea drenched with blood of the life it took. Don't go near it, don't swim in the water, don't try to sail on it. Make the gods happy, or they punish you. The story is about a girl, who does not want to go into the priesthood venerating these gods who kill all life if they misbehave. Though she cannot escape the fate of being turned into a priestess, she can try to alter the system. Which she is going to do in the trilogy.

Other inspirations get to me, when I'm listening to a song. I had great Steampunk ideas listening to Spetsnaz (especially the song "'Faustpakt"). The book in progress is now called *The mechanical city.*

I find it very helpful to write ideas down.

Write them down, either in a book or in a blog or on your computer/iPad, whatever works best for you. I always have a little notebook with me wherever I go and my phone, just in case.

Write ideas down!

I know from other creative people, that they sometimes really sit down with a paper or pad and write down ideas. So you might have to take some time, relax, and let your mind roam free to find ideas you connect to.

Sit down, take a cup of tea or coffee, whatever you love to drink or eat, and turn on music you love. Sit somewhere comfy and let your mind drift. Dream of beautiful things, of a land, you would love to see and visit. However unrealistic or realistic, write it down, just sketches, just words, you don't have to write a lot (you may, if you want to though).

Do you dream a lot? If yes, write them down, these are inspirations just waiting to be put into a novel. Some dreams of mine are still waiting to be written into a novel. If not, try to dream more. There are some good books about dreaming and lucid dreams. Look for them and try them.

What are the inspirations you get, when you see the following pictures?
Jot them down

Your ideas:

Your ideas:

Your ideas:

Your ideas:

Your ideas:

Write down 10 ideas to write a
short story or book about

3

THE LONG WRITING AND CREATING PROCESS

So now, looking at your ideas, you see what genre I will be writing in, what brings me to the question you will be facing, either before or after you had your idea.

What genre to write in?

There are a lot of different genres you can base your story in:

- love story or romance

- science fiction

- fantasy

- crime or criminal detective

- horror

- children's book

- reality based

- erotic

I love writing fantasy novels, and I love writing and reading love-stories. So I normally mix those two together. I always have a bit of a love story going on in my stories. I don't think I could really write a credible character without having him or her fall in love with someone.

If you love writing it, there will be thousands of people out there that will love what you write. There is no right and no wrong. Write what you want to write about. There are a lot of kids to read your children's book, or women and men who just love to see a happy ending.

Why not write just that?

Why not make them happy and live off something you love and they obviously love?

Just do it.

Haters will hate, but lovers will love!

Highlight what you love or add
different genres to the list
above

Writing style

First of all you will have to decide what you write: a short story, a book, a novel, a theatre play, a screenplay, or maybe none of the above? In what tense will you be writing? What is your way of writing?

Shortstory or Trilogy?

I cannot give you the ultimate advice on that. But it is nothing wrong with writing a short story. Several short stories could be put into a book. If you want to write a book, a book about 200 normal pages is a good length for a first timer. My first book had over 600 pages. So please, if you want to write a longer story, don't be frustrated if it gets shorter, that's fine. A lot of people are scared reading a big book. If your write a big book, like over 600 pages, think of parting it. A big book with parts, like a trilogy, sells better than one big book. Believe me.

Part a big book!
A trilogy always sells better

You will have your way and that is the perfect way for you to write. So do it.

Every length is right - it just has to be perfect for you

Tenses

In what tense should you write? This does not mean Victorian or 22nd century, which would be choice of genre or story, but present tense or past tense. The ordinary book out of your bookshelf will be written in past tense. I think, that is the easiest way to write and to read a story. But I know from books I have read that newer authors sometimes use the present tense. If you feel more comfortable to do it in that tense, just go ahead. If you are not sure, take your favourite book and see what it is written in or just try writing a short story in either tenses and decide on what you like best. Just do not mix them. Absolutely do not mix them.

Decide on one tense and stick to it

Point of view

There are several ways to write your story.

- third person point of view (limited)
- third person point of view (omnipotent)

CONTENTS

- second person point of view

- first person point of view

Either of them is fine.

Second person point of view is only used in non-fiction writing though. You tell someone what you did. Perfect for scientific writing.

Third person point of view can be either limited or omnipotent. I opt for the omnipotent version more or less all the time in books, because it gives you the option to tell the story out of the view of every character of the story. So you are able to have to main persons, like protagonist and antagonist, and are able to write about each of their action and plots against each other.

This is the most used point of view technique in fictional books.

The limited third person point of view is limited to just one character and normally without access to thoughts and experiences.

First person point of view books can be very charming, as they are a bit more personal, but of course limited to just that character. I opt for that when writing my short stories.

See what speaks to you or your story concept the most and use it. Really, all of them are fine.

Chapters

I like using chapters in a book, I think it gives structure to your story and I like reading the table of contents and anticipating what might come. But you do not have to use them. One of my all time favourite book writers, Terry Pratchett, very seldom used chapters. There are different options to structure your book.

- You can opt for chapters to give your book an ordinary structure. If you choose to have chapters, name them. Either it is just a short word that has something to do with that chapter, a number or a longer sentence, that describes that chapter a bit more. I would recommend not to be too clear with you chapter naming. It takes away the fun to know what will happen in the next chapter and spoils the book. Always start that chapter on a new page. Preferable actually on a right page, an odd numbered.

- If you think, your book is actually not only separated into chapters, but also into big parts, then do that as well. A good number of parts is always the magical number three: beginning, high tide, and end.

- You can separate different chapters with a little star or dot if you want to and refrain from naming chapters. You would not start a new page with a new chapter in that case.

- If you opt for not having any chapters whatsoever, you absolutely should opt for paragraphs though. You need a bit of structure to make the story readable.

Elaborate or intense?

Everyone has his or her unique writing style. There is no right or wrong. But there is readable and not readable.

Tolkien for example has a very elaborate and descriptive writing style. He goes into every detail of every bush. There are people who love reading this and love having a world put together around them with every sentence.

But there is the other style, which I call the intense style, because it does describe some things, but leaves a lot of room for the reader's imagination and concentrates on the action. Terry Pratchett would be an example of the intense style.

Either of the styles is readable, just not for everyone. I love the intense style. I have lots of imagination and if you tell me how to picture someone or something you may not be able to change my view of it, no matter how detailed the description is. So I tend not to read such stories. It doesn't matter which one you choose. It is most likely going to be a mixture of them anyway. Choose the style, you like writing and like reading. Test them on other people; read to them. If more than just one person says, it is too long, too elaborate or too short and too fast, think about it. If you still love it: don't change it. It is your story, your baby.

I will give you examples of different writing

styles to give you a better idea of how different they might be.

First of all, I want to show you the unreadable way or very artistic way. In German literature there was a strong period of expressionism during the 1900-1930. They wrote gorgeous poems and I love them, but their short stories are difficult. Maybe they are very interesting from an artistic point of view, but they are definitely not really *easy reading*. So if you aim to sell your book to the masses, you should not write like that:

I will give you a short (translated) example of an expressionist's (Gottfried Benn) writing:

> *Against tropic and subtropic influences, salt mines and rivers of lotus, caravans of Berber, yes, against the antipodes themselves is a ship's belly; on a plain, which is lined with mimosa, empties reddish resin, a slope between lime marl, the fat clay. Europe, Asia, Africa: bites, deadly reaction, horned vipers; at the end of the jetty a house of pleasure steps to greet the newly arrived, in the desert, quiet, stands the sultan chicken. - It was quiet still, yet the olive happened to it.*

This is, what I consider to be unreadable, the German version is just as unreadable. This is not a translation error.

So, how could you write a story then? I will give you three different versions of the same scene. These are three different approaches of writing to the point, where I would stop. So take a look at the scenes, consider the differences and decide on what kind of writing style would suite you most. Which you liked reading the most and which you think you can write as well.

Very short, almost unreadable:

Hagfast called for Time's help. A bright light appeared and the creature made a sound. The insect burned and then the creature was merely bones and dust.

Hagfast saw the danger was over. He saw Kyron and some other injured soldiers.

Hagfast kneeled at Kyron's side and cursed. That was it! He could feel the life draining out of Kyron.

"I presume that's it?"

"Yes, I can't undo the harm it has done. I am too late. Please forgive me, my friend"

"I do, Hagfast, I always did. Keep my memory close to you."

The priest took his friend into his arm and held him close. Just two blinks afterwards, Kyron took his last breath.

This is just very short and therefore almost unreadable. It lacks emotion; it lacks description of the surroundings. It lacks everything, which makes a story engaging.

More descriptive:

Hagfast raised his arms and called for Time's help. A bright light appeared and the creature made a sound. The insect burned, it shrank in size and seemed to dry out. It took only some blinks of the eye and the creature was merely bones crumbling to the ground.

Hagfast closed his eyes and looked around him. As he hoped, the magic just evaporated and left their bodies and the fortress. When he opened his eyes again and gestured at a nearby soldier, that the danger was over, he saw him pointing at Kyron and some other badly injured soldiers. In an instant Hagfast was kneeling at Kyron's side and felt for his injuries. He cursed quite loudly, as he saw, what the timeless monster had done. That was it! He could feel the life draining out of Kyron.

"I presume that's it?" asked Kyron.

"Yes, I can't undo the harm it has done. I am too late. Please forgive me, my friend," mumbled Hagfast.

"I do, Hagfast, I always did. Keep my memory close to you." Kyron tried to open his mouth again.

The priest took his friend into his arms and held him close. He felt the power of life leave the body of his friend. Just two blinks afterwards, Kyron took his last breath.

This is more descriptive. You get an idea about the scene and what is happening. There

are some emotions, some descriptions of move-
ment and some words describing how someone
says something, so you can imagine, what the
person feels or maybe even thinks.

Even more descriptive:

Hagfast raised his arms high into the air and called for Time's help. He drew the power of his belief out of the surrounding area, felt the power surge through his body, and unleashed it upon the monster right in front of him. A bright light appeared and the creature made an awkward sound. The insect arms burned in holy fire, the non-human legs seemed to shrink. The whole creature withered away. It shrank in size and seemed to dry out, as if years of aging hit it all in one moment. It took only some blinks of the eye and the creature was merely reduced to bones crumbling to the ground. When they hit the ground they disintegrated into dust and were blown away by a light breeze.

Hagfast closed his eyes and looked around him. He tried to see what happened to all the other timeless creatures, although he did not have the power of his partner Kyron to support him. As he hoped, the magic just evaporated and left their bodies and the fortress. Cutting the root of the problem had been a very good idea. When he opened his eyes again and gestured at a nearby soldier, that the danger was over, he saw him pointing at Kyron and some other badly injured soldiers.

In an instant Hagfast was kneeling at Kyron's side and felt for his injuries. He cursed quite loudly, as he saw, what the timeless monster had done. It had ripped apart every muscle Kyron needed for moving, his heart was raptured as well. That was it! With all his powers, he was unable to help his beloved friend. He could feel the life draining out of Kyron. It was too late.

"I presume that's it?" asked Kyron with a very faint and knowing smile.

"Yes, I can't undo the harm, it has done. I am too late. Please forgive me, my friend," mumbled Hagfast with tears in his eyes.

"I do, Hagfast, I always did. Keep my memory close to you." Kyron tried to open his mouth again, but it would not work. Pleading eyes looked at Hagfast.

The priest took his friend into his arms and held him close. One last touch and one moment of closeness between the loving friends. He felt the power of life leave the body of his beloved and tried to guide him to the entrance of the everlasting circle of Time. Just two blinks afterwards, Kyron took his last breath. He passed away in the arms of Hagfast and would reunite with Time itself. Creator of everything.

Hagfast let go of his partner and composed himself for a long breath, and then he looked around to help other men in need. This death should not be wasted. He needed to work now, help, and heal all the others.

You probably now see the difference between the three examples. You could add as much description as you want to the third one. I would not really do a lot. But that is my writing style and you need to find the writing style, which suits you most.

Whatever writing style resonates
best with you is your perfect
style

It is totally up to you, to find
YOUR style. Go on. Do it now!
Check other books and try to
find, what you like the most

4

YOUR WORLD

And now, you start writing your book. Yes, start now. There is nothing fancy you need, a computer and a typing program or a piece of paper and a pen. That is all you need - as comes to material. Creativity, ideas, and an open mind are needed for sure, too.

You have written down your story ideas. Whatever sings to you the most, pick it and work with it the next chapter. So we can start to write your first book! You will do it, I am totally positive about that.

When you have your idea, you need to draft a world you write your novel in. Either it is in the real world we are living in or it is a fantasy world.

For both ways, there is a way to design it. You have to research for the real world or create your own world.

First I want to explain to you, how to fabricate your fictional world and then, how you research for a novel written on this planet.

Your fictional world

First of all you should decide if it is going to be a world with humans, solely humans or only aliens. Aliens means anything that is not human, like elves, cat people, lizard man or alien such as in any science fiction you can think of (good and bad).

You are free to design anything that is thinkable as your world. But I give you an advice.

Keep it plausible

That means: try to stay in the rules of physics. Humans are creatures of habit, so your reader will tend to believe your world when it stays plausible.

There is no harm in including gods, magic, different technology or alien races. But it has to be believable, somehow.

So how do you create a plausible and believable world?

Try to mimic cultures and systems people know. A lot of fantasy novels are placed in a world that mimics an ideal world. With swords, kings, and of course magic and witches.

The trick is to take something everybody knows and alter it just enough to make it fantastic, but not too much so that it's unrecognisable.

So, if you create a world, give it mountains, and an ocean somewhere, some rivers, and trees. But those trees don't have to look like normal trees, change their appearance. Maybe they bloom in the winter. No leaves, but full of crystal blue blossoms twinkling with ice.

Or give your human looking figures a connection to a god and magic powers derived from that bond.

I love to extend the range of hair colours and eye colours, as I always wanted to have a different one.

I like inventing different creatures, too. I tend to stick to a humanoid form as that helps the plausibility of my world.

I know that there are infinite ways of life to form, but to write a credible one, the reader must be able to identify with them somehow. As we are humanoid beings, creating aliens with key features of that, helps the reader to do so. If you think of fantasy or science fiction novels or films you will find that to be true.

Even magic has to follow logical rules. So do yourself a favour and create a magic system. Either based on different elements, gods or vocations. If you want to, create a spellbook. You can write that down before you write your story. I wouldn't, as I am lazy, but I would write it down along the way. But you really should keep track of the wordings you use (if any) or the way your magic or godly powers work.

Keeping track is essential for plausibility and credibility

You might forget what spell you used at the beginning of your book, but your readers won't.

Not only keeping track of your magic system helps, but keeping track of your belief system as well. Write a hierachy down. You are going to forget otherwise.

Another important bit is:

Draw a map of your world

You don't have to be an artist to draw a map of your world. Just draw some countries, where are borders, where are cities, where are rivers, mountains, dense forest, or swamp.

With that you have consistency in describing your countries and cities. It also helps you to keep track, if your characters travel. Scribing the journey and the landscape. Don't worry about the look. You can always give your drawing to an artist, that makes it nice for a book to publish. I included two maps here from a book I wrote. As you can see: not overly pretty, but it works. The first one was the first draft, so I knew, where my cities where. You might see changes and drawing in the map. The second one was a nicer version, so you know where forests are etc.

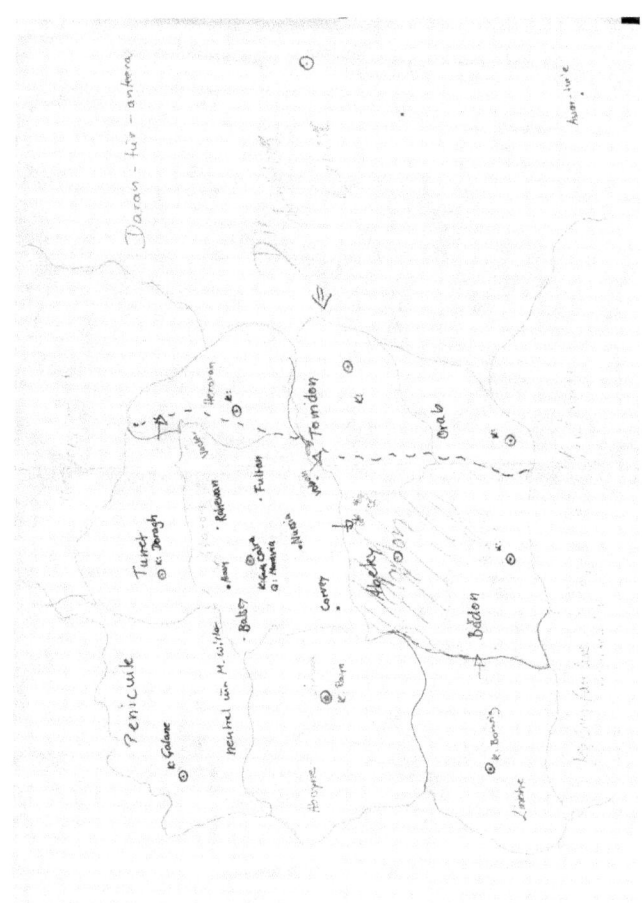

39

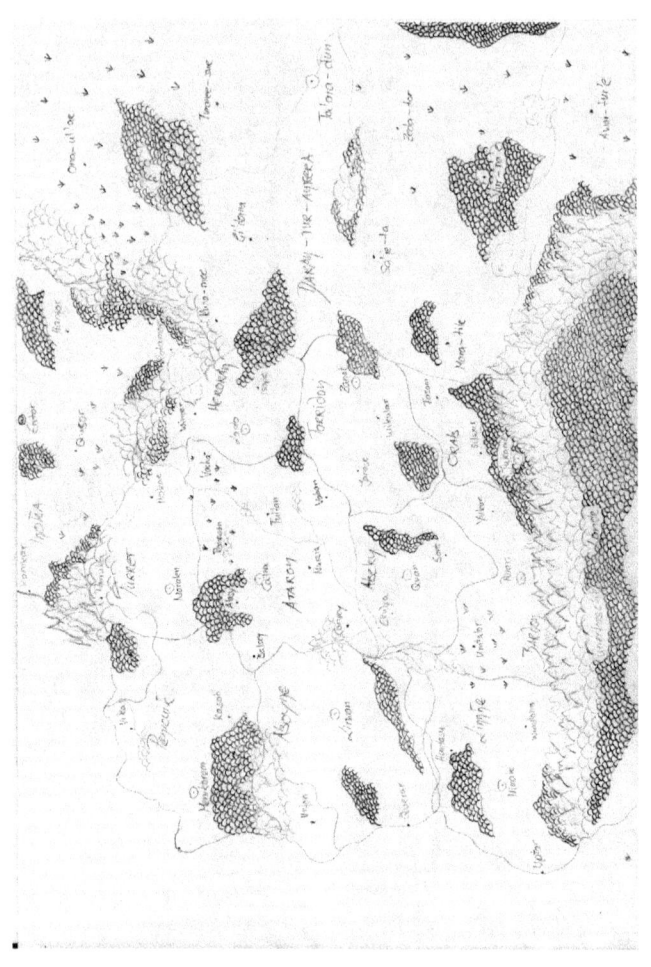

World

Countries

Belief system(s)

Level of technology

Notes / Wars / Problems

❀

❀

❀

❀

Country

Capital City

Ruler

Important persons

Landscape

Belief System

❀

❀

❀

City

Name of city

Ruler

Important persons

Important buildings

House design and layout

❋

❋

❋

Cult

Name of god

Hierachry of Priests or similar

Important persons

Relics

Core Belief

❂

❂

❂

Do your research

If you write in the known world, you should do an extensive research on the time period you are writing in and the cities your novel is based in. I recommend visiting these cities and not only looking everything up on google. That might give you an idea, but just an idea. It is always different to walk the streets you are describing.

If you go for the earth as a planet and the humans on it, another thing is quite necessary. Getting to know the physics and biology of this planet. You cannot write a computer novel with IT specialties without having any clue about IT or computer. If you don't have any idea about that, get somebody to explain it to you.

The same applies of you write about something in the past. You need to get the history right. If you don't, the people who know a lot about this time period will smash you. Do yourself a favour and get help or do your research. Read current literature and don't just read the popular works, but try to research some real scientific books at your nearest university.

Research libraries and
universities near you. Take
pictures of interesting things
you see where you live or when
you are travelling

5

ENTICING CHARACTERS

There are a couple of things, which make your good story an awesome story: enticing characters, enchanting worlds, and intriguing dialogues.

So, lets start with the characters. How do you create an enticing character?

You should decide, what their purpose in the story is. Normally that comes without thinking because you are creating that character for a special purpose. This purpose might actually influence the visual appearance you want to give your character.

You should have a visual idea of the character. What does he or she look like? Decide on the gender of your character. Decide, what kind of person it is. Is it a human or a non human being? If it is a human being: what hair colour does your character have? What eye colour? How tall is your character? Is he/she big or skinny? Does he or she have anything unusual, like a scar or birthmark? If you are a talented artist, you could draw your character to give you a better view of the person.

These are the visual traits. When you have them, visualise the character in front of your mental eye and think of the voice he or she might have. If you hear that voice, write down some characteristics of that voice.

Now think of your character and give him or her character traits. What flaws does he or she have? What merits does she or he have? Anything, that he or she is neurotic about? For example, your character could indulge in chastity to be a better regent and not to be distracted by a lover or emotions.

What kind of affiliation does he or she have? You could write down, from which country he or she comes or what group he or she belongs to.

You should think of antagonists as characters as well. If this is your antagonist (the *evil* person of your story), then the protagonist is the antagonist. This is just a matter of point of view really.

On the next page I made a character template or sheet for you. Use it, if you want to, or add as much information as you need.

Charactersheet

Name

Appearance

merrits

flaws

Main goal

function in book

Antagonist

Notes

❇

The same rule that applied for the creation of your world applies here:

Plausibility and consistency

To achieve that, we should delve into human behaviour for a moment. As I stated before, humans are creatures of habit. If your character is human, he or she should behave like one.

So what is the *normal* behaviour of a human being?

A human is a creature of habit. The ordinary human doesn't like change and he doesn't embrace new things easily. So new beliefs, new systems or a new ruler are seldom easily accepted.

Every human being and actually every character, needs a motivation to do something. There are as many motivations as stars in the universe. The strongest ones are the emotional ones like: love or fear.

Here is a list of the most common ones.

- Love

- Power

- Fear

- Anger

- Hatred

- Revenge

- Seeking Justice

- Family

- Greed

- Lust

- Survival

With these motivators in mind, you are now able to give your character a reason to do something. Every character will have their way of achieving their main goal enforced by their motivator.

Some might calculate every move they make and every step their opponent takes before hand. Your readers might not see or know what that character's motivator is except calculating. if that's so: you've done a brilliant job in describing that particular character.

But you, as an author, should always be aware of the main motivator of all your characters.

Other than calculating the standard human being rather tends to express their motivator and so inspired actions through emotional acts. The majority of human beings isn't rational.

Unless you write about a non emotional race, you should give your character at least a bit of emotional acting.

A weak point is always a good idea. Every character ought to have one. It might be something that has happened in the past, it might be a fetish, a beloved one, a secret that would ruin their life if told.

Another thing your character might have is a flaw or maybe even more than one. Your character might be very impulsive or has difficulties bonding.

On the other hand your character should have merits. He or she could be very empathetic or a fast thinker.

With that package you have a credible character.

Every action of you character should be in keeping with his motivations and his goal. Don't spill everything at once. The reader should slowly discover every aspect of the character in your book. Keep the good bits and just lay some hints now and then.

Have fun with describing your character und enjoy the creation process.

6

STORYLINE

The main story

First of all, you need to create a storyline. This is a bit like a script for a movie, just for your book. You have your idea. When you have your idea, your world and at least a protagonist and even better an antagonist, you start with writing down the goal of your book.

When you have done that, you write how to reach that goal.

Next you fill in the gaps.

What has to be achieved for your main character to reach that goal.

And on the other hand: what has your antagonist to do to reach his goal?

It always helps, if you write little goals, like steps your characters need to achieve to come closer to the closure of your book.

That could look like that:

Mainplot Moravia:

- **Moravia married an abusive king and wants to get rid of him.** (plot of the story)

- Moravia has to find someone that will murder her husband

- She finds out, she is not only human and her husband isn't either, so blunt murder is not an option any longer

- In finding out she is not human either, she also finds her ally helping her to end her pain and fulfil her destiny (save her country)

- They plan their attack

- Make the king vulnerable

- Confront the king and kill him

- Save the country

- Collect all lose ends and round up the story

You can be as detailed as you want. If you struggle, write more details in your storyline, that helps a lot.

If you have more characters or protagonists and they have different stories, include them in that storyline, or make references to their storyline. So, a subplot in that book would be the one of Cramond, the person helping Moravia.

Subplot Cramond:

- **Got mentally connected to Garth and wants to rid of this connection in order to live freely again (main goal)**

- Finds Moravia and discovers her to be the chosen one to free his country and kill the destroyer (her husband)

- Needs to bond with her in order to break the connection to his punisher

- Helps her to use her magic powers

- Becomes her lover and only true love (gifted by goddess)

It is totally up to you to write this as a document on your computer or on a notebook. I love notebooks, because they can lie next to me while I type on my computer. But that is just a matter of liking. Bulletjournals are awesome for that.

On the next page, I give you an outline of a storyline, to you use as an inspiration.

Storyline - Sketch

Goal

Protagonist

Antagonist

Outline

⚘

⚘

⚘

⚘

Write 5 of your story ideas as a
storyline - short but to the
point

Where do I start?

Good stories are simple, untangled. Take one of the best selling stories on the market: Lord of the Rings. "One ring has to be destroyed, before it destroys the world." That is the sole purpose of the trilogy. The rest is just the long walk with several obstacles. Without the simple purpose of destroying the powerful ring, it would be a tangled, unreadable mess.

The fleshing out of that story is the part, which makes it readable and interesting.

The right starting point makes it good as well. Imagine that story starting after the ring is destroyed. What a bore. Great idea, you have of a land with great disasters that have happened - but yes, they are history. The elves will leave Middle Earth, all is well - nothing interesting happens. You can have stuff in flashbacks, but not the whole story. That is just too complicated and too mixed up.

I will show you, what I mean with a simple idea by demonstrating it on a novel I am currently writing. I use work titles, which do not necessary end up being the book title. Mostly it is the name of the main character.

The idea is a creature, that is half human and half wolf, has to be turned back to being just human. That is the very sketchy idea of that book.

So, where do I start writing the story then? Do I start with the mother of the creature? Well

I could, but that would mean long years of childhood of the creature, well girl to be precise, growing up. The idea is, that the wolf part becomes evident, when the girl becomes a woman. Do I want to write all of that? Does this sound fascinating to read? Well...no, it doesn't. So I will start when she is a woman.

To make things more interesting, I won't let the reader know, what the real problem is. But I will actually start with the hero of the story, the man who will free her from the spell. He is a priest, a priest of time, and he will be sent on a mission to see what is happening. There are rumours and problems with creatures and unusual occurrences. He will find her as the source of the problem. He will find out, that she is against the natural order and against all the principles of his faith. He ought to kill her - but he falls in love with her.

That is the story sketched out a bit more. For me, that is enough to start writing. I have things to aim for and start the writing process. To have a better overview, I recommend writing this down as a sort of sketch. So you know, what comes up next.

Write down steps and pieces of
your story to give you a guidance
to write by

Well, with the first chapter or prologue, I suggest. Decide where you want to start your story. Then decide, if you want to add a prologue, which might be earlier in the story, than your actual beginning. I did that with three of my books and I think it is nice, but not necessary.

Start with your first scene: either with a description where the characters are or plunge into a conversation. Either is cool.

Choose your starting point, create an idea in your head and write. It is necessary to choose a starting point you would like to read. Don't load yourself with too much stuff. It is not interesting in writing about everything that has happened. Flashbacks are okay, or letting the main character find out, what has happened to the world. They could find out, what their destiny is. But that is so much better, if the reader discovers it together with the protagonist.

Storyline - details

Main plot

main goal of protagonist

secondary goal

important subplots

further details

❁

❁

❁

❁

❁

Storyline - Plot Antagonist

main goal

important characters

secondary goal

further details

*

*

*

*

*

Storyline - Subplot One

Character plot

main goal

secondary goal

further details

❀

❀

❀

❀

❀

Storyline - Subplot Two

Character plot

main goal

secondary goal

further details

❀

❀

❀

❀

❀

Storyline - Subplot Three

Character plot

main goal

secondary goal

further details

*

*

*

*

*

The importance of these sheets about the storyline and the notes you make is:

Keeping track

If you don't do that, you will loose the overview of your story. You will tangle yourself with details and wrong story endings.

Continuity is of essence

Another important thing you need to keep track of, is time. Not your time writing, but the time in the book. If you describe weather or temperatures in your world, it is essential, that you know what time of the year it is. So write that down. I tend to make a little calendar. Write down the months of my year (I opted for twelve months so far in my books, but that is totally up to you), and note what happens then. The year doesn't have to start in winter in your book, as is normal in the northern hemisphere, but could start in summer or autumn or spring.

So draw yourself a sort of calendar or a timeline to keep track of what time of the year it is. It comes in handy to write down, what happens on that timeline or at least important bits that correlate with your storyline.

Keep writing things down and make
them pretty. You will love
coming back to your notes and use
them

7

SCENES AND DIALOUGES

My best advice is:

Every scene has to have a purpose

Every single one

If your character enters a tavern and starts talking to someone, it has to have a reason. Great idea to go to a tavern and have a drink, but what happens there? Interesting talk?

So, if your character walks into the tavern and you start writing, what he or she drinks, he or she needs to talk about something or happen to meet somebody. When you let a character walk into a tavern, he should have a purpose. He needs to have an important conversation, meet somebody who is important for the storyline or do something interesting.

Let your characters roam free in your book. Let them have a choice and remember: every scene needs a purpose. Every scene. If you keep that in mind, your story will evolve, and progress, and become a good story.

So, how do you actually write a good scene?

Feel it

Sounds funny, but I am serious. You have to feel the situation. It is fine, if you imagine a situation, but when you feel it, you live it and will describe it better and more realistic.

If you feel the situation and know what your character feels, what he thinks, what he wants, what his inner needs are, you will be able to write that. If you write a scene, while feeling just what your character feels and write, what you would say being in that situation, your character and your dialogs will be so much more credible.

You have to become the character. The problem is: you have to be every single one of your characters. So, in every story, there will be a part of you in every character you write. In some characters, there will be more of you, in some less. That is fine and normal. That is why it sometimes really hurts to kill a character.

The more you can become the person you write about, the better it is for the story. And in this way, your characters will be free in your

70

story. It actually might feel as if they are deciding, what they do next and not you. I love it, when that happens. My main story will never change, but little plot twist will pop up and that makes the story so much better in my opinion - so much more credible!

So, here is an inspiration for you for a scene to write:

Close your eyes. Imagine a dark room, with no windows. Can you feel the cold floor under your feet? Can you feel the darkness around you? The unevenness of the stone floor? The draft, that comes through the thick wooden door blocking the only way out? See the woman kneeling on the floor? Waiting for her execution? Feel her despair? Her pain? So young and yet to die? See the colour of her hair, the eyes, and the clothes she is wearing? Yes? Can you imagine that? Great! You are where you need to be. Now you are in the perfect mood to write the scene.

And now: Write that scene

Awesome. You wrote your first scene. I am so proud of you!

Now I will give you my idea of that scene (actually the prologue of my second book *Ray*):

It was quiet. No sound reached the ears. The room was dark, no windows, no candles were lighting the room. On the cold, stone floor a woman was kneeling, as there was no furniture, nowhere to sit in this barren room. She was wearing a thin, but lovely red dress. Her blond locks were long and untamed. A tear formed in one of her bright eyes and ran along her cheek. Quietly she was awaiting her destiny. They would come for her soon enough.

She had had so many plans, had wanted to do so much with her eighteen winters. Travel, enjoy, just being free. But nothing like that was going to happen. She was awaiting her sacrifice. She would be dead this very night. Join him in the everlasting gardens of stars.

Another tear ran down the other cheek and another one. She brushed them away with her sleeve and tried to calm herself down a bit. It was so wrong. HE had wanted her sister, not her.

She twitched, when she heard the cumbersome steps on the stones in front of the massive wooden door. They came nearer and nearer and the young woman closed her eyes. "Farewell world," she thought and stayed where she was slightly shivering. This was the beginning of her end.

The heavy wooden door was opened with a loud creaking and squeaking noise. It scraped on the stone floor and rattle the more it moved.

"It is time," said a calm and friendly men's voice. "Come on, Coligny, please."

"Yes, father," Coligny mumbled with a muffled voice due to her tears. She rose slowly and faced her father. She would follow him to be executed in the name of their god.

You can do it, too. And I hope, you have an idea now, what you want to write about. I bet you will be having trouble along the way somewhere (as do I have now and then, too), so in chapter 10 "Troubleshooting", I gladly share my troubleshooting methods with you.

As you wrote that short, little story, do you have an idea of what your first scene is going to be like? Can you feel it? If yes, start writing it. Don't keep it in you - let it run free.

Writing dialogues

Now that you know, what your characters look like, how they move, the way they talk, and you learned, how to write a scene in general, you should learn how to write a dialogue. Dialogues enhance your book. They are a vital part of the story and make it awesome.

As I told you before in writing a scene, every scene has to have a purpose. The same applies to dialogues. If they say "Hi!" to each other, the purpose was greeting each other. With spoken words, purpose is easier than with a whole scene. I am pretty sure you will get the hang of it quite easy. So what makes up a good dialogue?

Authenticity

and

Consistency

If your character talks in a certain way and nothing out of the order happened, you should not change the way he or she talks and behaves. You should be consistent with what you write about some of your figures in the story.

Authenticity is a lot harder. Your characters need to talk like actual people. Sounds easy enough, but it is harder, than you think.

Like describing a scene, it comes in handy to become your character while writing the dialogue. That means you have to think like your character in order to let him or her speak in the way he or she would. A born fighter would probably not use high fashion words, but tends to talk more practically, which does not mean he has to be dumb. A born princess however would always refrain from talking too much like the lower class. She never would have been taught to talk like that.

Stylistically it helps to put describing words after your direct speech. How does a character say that, with what tone. Let your characters not only talk to each other, but let them do something. If you talk to somebody, you might scratch your chin, drink a sip of tea or anything similar. Thus making your story so much more like real life and it helps the reader to connect to the protagonist and the story itself.

So, when you are able to feel your character, feel the scene, you will be able to write awesome stories and enticing novels.

8

PRACTICAL TIPS

Here is some advice on what techniques or methods you should and could use when writing a book: from technical aspects like programs to organisational things.

Paper, Computer, Apps

Now up to the part of: how do I do that practically.

Basically there are two ways of doing it: writing by hand or typing it. If you write it by hand, either you or normally someone else will have to type it into a program. I know of one current writer who actually does that (W. Hohlbein), but I would not recommend that at all.

The choice of the program you will be typing in, depends on how and if you want to publish your books.

If you already have a publisher, they will mostly tell you how they want it, so do as they tell you.

If you don't have a publisher yet, which I presume, use the alternative to self publish your book. Amazon for examples has a great self-publishing tool, which allows you to print it, too.

Like CreateSpace, with which this book was created. They recommend using Microsoft word actually. I found that word crashes if you write to elaborate and long texts. Editing is such a pain, that I just totally cannot recommend that.

Apple's pages works nice, too, and can be easily converted into an epub format, which works beautiful with Amazon. You can use pdf's with CreateSpace, which allows you to imbed background images. It grants you more freedom designing your book.

I love using LaTeX with which this book was created. This is a professional writing tool for scientific books and great for including graphics, mathematic writing, and also just text with professional, plain layout. It comes with Apple OS and with Linux, it is not preinstalled on Windows but easy to install. Just google it, there are tons of sites for it including help forums. Springer uses that for scientific publishings. LaTeX though is rather a programming language like html and therefore not really easy going. If you are good with html or any languages like that, give it a try - it's for free!

There are other writing softwares as well, such as Scrivener or the editor Vellum. You should really have a look around to find, what suits you and your needs the most.

There are a thousand apps (okay, maybe hundreds) for doing an ebook, like iAuthor on Mac. They are great for sketching things down and getting them published for free. There is blurb, bod, or any other publishing on demand services.

Go, what feels best for you. If you want to do an e-course for free and just bring your book out into the world: go for them!

If you have the skills or someone to help you, you can always put your book into InDesign and really make a cool pdf of it. But, InDesign is not for free and you need a lot of skills in using it the right way. Amazon actually accepts pdfs, but kindle readers of course cannot process any background graphics, so keep it simple, if you publish an ebook.

```
Be creative and out of the box
  You will get sales that way
```

Work pace and deadlines

I get asked a lot about a good way to finish novels, how many pages or words to write a day. So, your work pace and deadlines is up next.

There are different strategies to write a book. You will have to find yours. I'll tell you, what works best for me and what other strategies I know of.

I tried the *Terry Pratchett* strategy and write 500 words each day. Good idea, inspiring, I love it. I think, it is a great one. It is a great way not to have too much pressure and just keep on writing, keep on going, and finish that book. So I highly recommend that strategy.

The other strategy would be, to write whenever you have time and feel the need to write. Problem with that is, that you will have a hard time to meet any deadlines. Believe me, if there is a deadline you will do almost anything but write that book. If this is just a hobby for you, then this is fine. If you want to live off your writing, you should not opt for that.

The third method, the method I am using, is to sit down on regular days and write. Normally, I write around three to five days a week for at least five to eight hours a day. I don't know how many pages I am writing on these days, but I get a whole lot done and ready. I am not always totally creative, but on these days I just edit something.

First thing you should do, is find out when you are most creative.

- In the mornings?

- Under the shower?

- At night with all the starry stars out?

That is the time you should write. It does not matter if that is an hour before breakfast or if it is late at night before you go to bed. If you feel good and creative, that is the only thing that matters.

How much time are you willing to spend on your project book?

If you have a time limit per day or week, use it.

If you don't, try to write every day, every second day, or every Thursday, and have a look at how much you write. Take the average and that is your page or word goal.

When are you creative?
Analyse and write it down

How much time do you want to
spend writing?

Write down a realistic writing goal!

What about deadlines then? Well, I don't like deadlines, but I know, a realistic deadline will actually work with me or at least encourage me of doing more and use my time more efficiently. I still don't usually give myself a strict deadline. But having a reading of your book might really do miracles (it does to me every time).

If you give yourself a deadline, keep it realistic! That is an important part. If you try to write a novel in a month, you won't finish it. But you'll have successfully depressed yourself with that. Not finishing on time AND not keeping your deadline.

Writing a good novel costs time. So a realistic deadline would be: write the first chapter in the next two months. So there is plenty of room for life to get in the way with your goal, but you can still, easily keep your goal. If you notice, that you are a fast writer, you can set closer deadlines. If you see, that it takes you longer, your baby is often sick or your job is too demanding, give yourself a longer deadline. Don't be too cruel to yourself; be kind.

Workplace

To be able to work and write consistently you should consider arranging for a workplace for your writing. It is work after all, even if you are not paid directly.

So, find a place, where you can really concentrate and work. If it is at your dining table, go for it. If it is in a café, do it.

But I recommend to you a real desk and a lovely corner or even better, your writing room. I have a shared study with my partner. My desk is directly in front of a large window, so I can look out, enjoy the blue sky and hear the birds singing. Sometimes I can witness a storm or the rain falling. Either I listen to music or nature while I write. Sometimes I have a documentary running in the background. I like it, when somebody talks to me while I am alone. My workspace is decorated with things I love. So my recommendation is: make your space creative, comfy, and lovely. You should enjoy spending time there.

So, make space for your writing. If you squeeze it somewhere in between, it will always feel, like you are not allowing yourself to become a successful writer.

Take it seriously!

Write down hours, when you want to work.

Call it work!

9

DOS AND DON'TS

So there are some dos and some don'ts. Lets start with the don'ts.

Don'ts

Don't prewrite scenes

Just don't. I am going to explain to you why you really shouldn't prewrite scenes for further in the book. The time you'll get to it, in 99,9 % you won't be able to use it. It doesn't make the story easier; you don't have the puzzle pieces. You are just going to make it complicated for you.

Your storyline might be changing during the writing process, characters dead or changed in their attitude because it fits the plot. So, what you wrote, might never take place, because you had a different idea 50 pages before that.

I had a glorious idea for a scene somewhere 2/3 of my first book when I was in the first quarter of the book and I just *had* to write it. So

I did. The thing, I wrote about was sort of a fixture at that time, so what could possibly go wrong?

Well, that scene is not in the book. All the stuff that needed to have happened to lead to that scene just didn't. Pity, I like that scene, it was a strong one, but well, wasted energy. I wasted two days of work.

So don't.

Take my advice and save your energy. Don't waste your creativity. It is hard to write through a boring scene, but you'll make it. It might be safe to skip the ending of a love-making scene or just write yourself a note there "more details", but everything with a dialogue, discussion, and stuff - just don't. You don't know what your characters end up saying - if you do? Write it down! Write the damn scene.

Have critique kill your energy

Believe me, when you write a story or a book, just about everybody knows how to do it the right way and knows everything better. They will actually correct your sentences, tell you how to write, not how they like the story. No one would do that, if you'd coded something, but everybody can write, can't they?

Well no, they can't.

Or have they written a book? Kept through the struggle of 300 pages? Wrote a real story?

If they have, fine, they might as well correct you then, but *not* on the *way* you write.

Maybe make suggestions if you missed a loose end in the plot - which even if you keep track of everything, might happen, believe me. That happens to the best authors. That's fine! You want critique like that. That is positive critique, that actually helps you, brings you forward to doing something great.

All the other critiques: well, take, what brings you forward and ignore the people, which want to bring you down, because they are jealous of your idea or do not want you to succeed.

Rewrite other people's books

Don't read a book and say: "Oh, that is nice, I can write it better, I didn't like what the character did."

You may of course get inspiration out of that. Just like my inspiration of a girl wanting to be a knight is not a new idea. Why not? There are several books about that. Runaway bride is a theme ever so occurring. But take the inspiration and make your *own* story. Don't copy something. It won't get published: you just stole somebody's love, idea, and creativity. That's like stealing someone's baby.

Don't change mythology too much

There are some unwritten rules. Mythologies are respected. Like folklore is a fixture. A witch uses a broomstick to fly, but a wizard might teleport. He does not ride a broomstick.

You get what I mean?

It is nice to redefine stuff, like Doctor Who does a lot when revisiting the past. Queen Victoria and the werewolf blood in the line. Van Gogh was a beautiful episode as well. But there is stuff, which will polarise people: like wizards on brooms.

Feel free to write that stuff, bought a special person freedom and out of poverty, still I would not do that. There is so much you can invent and think of. Why change those things, why not invent something of your own, where you know what is right and you define the folklore. That is so much easier, so much more *less* trouble, but so much more *You*.

Dos

Let your characters roam free!

Some people look at me kind of strange, when I say: "My characters sometimes do what they want to."

Like: *You* are writing the book! That can't happen.

But my characters do have a mind of their own and I *love* that.

So, if you write a scene, and somehow end up writing something not quite what you wanted to, like turned right when you wanted to go straight ahead - that is a character doing what it wants to. I think a story absolutely needs that.

So, do yourself and your story a favour and just let them decide. This makes your stories so much more authentic. It will make your characters so much more credible, so much more vivid and lovable.

Get proof readers

It helps, if other people read your story. They have a different point of view on the story and will let you know, if they found any major flaws. Even giving you a different view on the story, how it feels and what they think should happen.

Make sure, they know what to do. No correcting of your way of writing, just the story itself and typos of course. You won't see your typos, missing verbs at the end of the book, because you know what you've written. What does help, too, is reading it aloud, what brings me to the next point of dos.

Do readings
(in private or on a fair)

It will scare the hell out of you, quite possibly, but it is worth it. Having an audience, which just wants to hear you and your story helps you to know, if your story is loved. It will be loved by you, but do other people love it, too? If they ask you later when it is going to be published... they are hooked. Job well done.

To do this is easy. Either you invite some of your friends at home to do a private reading, or you look for fairs to read at. I had several readings at the Feencon, a fair for roleplayers. They always enjoy a good fantasy story. Look for one, which does *not* charge you any money. I've never paid anything for the chance to read aloud. The Comic Con in the US might be a bit too big for starters, but you get my idea.

10

TROUBLESHOOTING

Here are some ideas to help you with the troubles that will come up sooner or later. If you follow all advice, there will be less trouble, but I can't promise you to never have any.

Keeping track

Most important of all: keep track of your characters, your names, the look, and the places they have been to. Sounds easy, but believe me, with a big novel, you will forget what your character did and thought on page 30. Especially if the character does not appear too often, you might even have another idea of his hairstyle, colour, or skin. I gave you a template to create of your characters. You could use it for keeping track as well.

I recommend a file or book for that. I like to use a very old school approach and write it down in a little book: one page for each character, land, or deity.

Jot down the height of a person, the hair colour and length, and overall appearance, anything that stands out, any detail, you might forget. I like to add anything of importance to the story there, too. Like "father of", "in love with", "doesn't know his past" - something like that. On my website, I have more sheets for keeping track of your world and story for free. Just hop on it and download it.

So every time, you are not sure if the kingdom of Ataron really has all that windy castles and lots of forest, just look it up.

Write down the story ideas and parts as well, so you do not lose track of something you once started somewhere. I admittedly forget about that part, but it really helps if you do it thoroughly.

I like the old school way, as it gives me the chance to take it with me everywhere I go and I have it just next to my computer and do not have to switch documents. I also sometimes write parts of the story, if I am not at home, on my iPad or on a piece of paper or another book. Therefore the old school version helps as well. But do it the way you want to do it, you have to work with it, no one else.

Getting stuck

Everybody gets stuck at some point. What to do then?

There are mostly two (maybe three) reasons to get stuck:

- boring scene, that is necessary, but just bores you to bits

- no idea how to bridge the now with the then. You know how the story in theory continues, but you don't know how to do it.

- you *really* don't know how to continue

I will try to give you some ideas how to cope with these situations.

Boring scenes

A boring scene doesn't mean, that it is boring to read, it is just a filler or a must have in between the stuff, you like and you want to write about. It is a necessary scene for the progression of the story or one character, so you need to write it, if you want to or not. Because, if it is an unnecessary scene and it is boring you - delete it.

I had such a boring scene in my first book. It was a marriage scene, which had to be written and all the conversations were important. So, what did I do? Well, I always wrote like a couple of sentences, got totally bored and stopped. I took a break, did some knitting and thought about other stuff. I returned to my story some hours later and wrote a couple of sentences again.

I was not fast and I complained a lot to other people about the scene, but I kept on writing. Not every day, though.

Take some time off, do totally different stuff. Structure your boring scene in different parts, so you have only a little bit to write, then the next step, so you have the feeling of achieving something. So, this is the list of the mentioned scene:

- describe getting the dress

- meeting with the priestess, talk about magic and Garth

- talk between Moravia and Jara

- last favour before marriage → death of Garth's heir

- ceremony

- party after ceremony, talk to Cramond about bonding

The funny part about the scene is: people love it. And *no one* thinks, that this scene bored me to bits.

Stuck

Well, that actually is a big problem, because it leaves you on the middle of a bridge and you can already see the other end, there are just some timber pieces missing. What really helps me is: put the book aside. Do something totally different for a while. Not just for some hours, but for a while really. If you have other ideas, start a different book, seriously. Come back after a time, when you really want to continue writing and read the whole book again to where you stopped. Normally you will have an idea how to continue. If you don't, you can repeat the stuff above.

If that all does not work, you are *really* stuck. You need to do something else.

Sketch your book idea down, write down: what you want to achieve, write everything down in short sentences, what is going to happen next. This should give you an idea how to proceed with the story and how to bridge the gap.

I give you an idea, of how I did it, when I was stuck with my second book. And I got really stuck for months.

idea: raise belief of ancient god

- Ray is fighter, sort of paladin of the god

- Ray used to be his lover over centuries, the reason he split up with the goddess

- Strakonta, regent in other country wants to keep the belief in his goddess against all odds

- Ries Connor - incarnation of god

- Coligny - his reborn high priestess

- Arkana - lover of Ray, sort of blessed or touched by the god? → define!

status quo:

- Coligny has risen from the dead to spread the belief among the people

- Arkana needs time alone

- Ries and Ray have a love affair as well (perfectly fine with Arkana)

That was status quo, when I got stuck. So this is, what I wrote after that, how the story was supposed to continue.

- Coligny will raise a belief in the underground and finds love in Gilead, the head of thieves

- Arkana will be kidnapped to devastate Ray

- Strakonta plotting against the kingdom Ray lives in in the background to stop the new belief

I did not write down much, when I got an idea. I stopped, where Ries and Ray where in her room and making out with each other.

The scene would be, Ray getting the news that Arkana was kidnapped, possibly in her room, while Ries has to hide (as she is acting as a boy at court). She heads off with Ries Connor to rescue Arkana. She is found out and brought to Strakontas court. So, after struggling, not knowing what to do, that actually helped me.

Sometimes it also helps talking to another person, sort of your muse. I told my girlfriend a lot about my stories and books and she was a great inspiration, although she did not actually need to say something. Just talking to a person sometimes does the trick for me.

If I think of new stories or like this one to continue, I mostly listen to music or just stare out of my windows. So, light a candle to get in a writing mood, listen to music you like, drink tea (or coffee), relax and push pressure aside. You will finish that story; you will find a way to write it. Maybe it takes some time longer, but it will come to you.

No story ideas

Okay, that is a difficult one for me actually. I am *never* out of ideas to write stuff. Never, and I really mean never. I think in my head there are 30 ideas waiting to be written, which really could be a good book and 50 more, which are more short stories, but nothing definite.

So, what if you do not have an idea?

Well, one reason might be: you are not a born writer. Maybe you are a born painter. I do suck at painting stuff greatly, though my mother is a painter and sculptor. Maybe you are a totally talented knitter or mechanic? Not everybody is meant to be a writer.

But if you feel the need to write and cannot find anything to write about, maybe you are looking into the wrong direction? Or try too hard?

- Ever thought of writing articles for newspapers?

- Garden magazines?

- Style guides?

- Or a book about your life, if it was very cool?

- A book about your granny?

- How to maintain a healthy living while owning a cat?

So, get yourself a pencil and write down everything you can think of to write about, what would interest *you*.

11

WISHES

All the best

So, my gorgeous soul, you have what it takes to write a good story, an enticing story, a story that people will love. Go ahead. Write it! Take your word out into the world! Tell the unwritten stories, let us build a forest out of books, a forest made of dreams unwritten and untold.

As a special treat for you and to thank you, that you bought my book and read through it, I will offer you here an email address to contact me for a one time free session to talk (skype) or type about your questions about your book writing.

awesomestories@erinhthorn.com

I'll be anticipating your emails, your stories, your ideas, and questions.

ERIN H. THORN

I'm a passionate, crazy and devoted author, writer, and artist. I'm part Australian and part German. Currently I live in Germany. I'm a mother of a beautiful son. Four cats roam my flat with my partner and me. They all inspire me greatly with their love, presence, and affection.

I graduated in German literature and old history at the university of Bonn and did a PhD in Scandinavian studies, too.

I worked ten years of my life as an event manager. I organised big events with lots of staff, music, and lovely catering. In that time I learnt to really focus on the important things, worked on time management, and succeeded in making my customers happy. It also helped me with marketing. The most beautiful part: I had to design awesome stories for some of these events to be played.

My last job, before becoming a full time author, was as a social media manager and e-learning teacher. Thus giving me the skill to fine-tune marketing and living my second passion: teaching.

My first passion has always been writing. As early as 13 did I write my first novel and the love for fantasy literature stayed with me all that time.

I prefer writing fantasy literature, poetry, and short stories.

I offer coaching and workshops for young authors to intensify their knowledge on book writing. I also help people to untangle from other creative blocks.

For further information, freebies or just news about me, my cats, and my art: visit my website or follow me on social media.

www.erinhthorn.com

Space for notes

Space for notes

Space for notes

Space for notes

Space for notes

Space for notes

Space for notes

Space for notes

Space for notes

Space for notes

Space for notes

Space for notes

Space for notes